GIANTS AND DEMONS

Bhasmalochana the Fiery-eyed Demon

SHUBHA VILAS

Om KIDZ
An imprint of Om Books International

The demon Bhasmalochana who lived in Patal Lok had special powers. Whomever he saw, would turn into ashes that very moment. He was also a friend of Ravana.

After Ravana abducted Sita and carried her away, Lord Rama attacked Sri Lanka to rescue his wife. A fierce battle took place between the two mighty armies.

Ravana's brother Kumbhakarna was killed by Rama's arrows. Ravana was wild with rage. That is when he sought the help of his friend Bhasmalochana to lead the army and fight against Rama.

Bhasmalochana immediately stepped in to fight on behalf of his friend, Ravana. Rama's monkey army was very confused when they saw only one man from the enemy side walking down to fight them.

This man walked confidently towards the waiting vanara army. He was not only alone, but also blindfolded! As the man came closer, the vanaras saw that the band that covered his eyes was glowing. That is when the vanaras realised that they are facing Bhasmalochana, the demon who could burn with his vision!

The vanaras began to run helter-skelter. No one wanted to be around when this man removed his blindfold. Literally trampling each other, the terrified vanara army began to retreat.

There was only one question on everyone's mind. *What to do now? What will happen when Bhasmalochana removes his blindfold?*

As soon as Bhasmalochana removed his blindfold, the frightened vanaras saw his eyes shining like the noonday sun. In whichever direction he glanced, there was a flash of light, and a heap of ashes. Soon, across the battlefield, the vanaras were burning to ashes.

When Hanuman saw the ghastly scene, he started running. Everyone wondered, *Why is he running away? Without Hanuman, where was the hope to fight this demon?*

Suddenly, one vanara soldier shouted, 'Look! Look! Look where Hanuman has reached!'

Far away, they could see Hanuman climbing the fortress of Ravana. He had just jumped into the city. If he was running away, why was he running into the enemy camp? It was all a puzzle for the vanaras.

Suddenly, the vanaras saw their hero flying out of the fort balancing a plank with one hand and his tail. His other hand was navigating the flight. Rama and Lakshmana exchanged a knowing glance. Hanuman silently flew and landed right near Bhasmalochana. The vanaras hiding behind rocks, trees, or inside waterbodies were curious to know what Hanuman was up to.

Hanuman's tail lowered the plank in such a way that it came right in front of Bhasmalochana and blocked his vision. As soon as the plank landed on the ground, there was a classic blast. *BOOOM!*

The jubilant vanara army jumped out and came running towards Hanuman, their saviour. Those who still didn't understand what exactly happened, turned behind to see what that plank was.

It was a mirror!

Hanuman had made Bhasmalochana see himself! He had used his brains to defeat a dangerous enemy.

Bhasmalochana was now a heap of ashes.